Christian

FOUNDATIONS

Christian FOUNDATIONS

A DISCIPLESHIP COURSE
FOR NEW CHRISTIANS

MICHAEL GREEN

MONARCH
BOOKS

Published by Monarch Books
an imprint of
Lion Hudson IP Ltd
Wilkinson House, Jordan Hill Road,
Oxford OX2 8DR, England
Email: monarch@lionhudson.com
www.lionhudson.com/monarch

ISBN 978 0 85721 876 6
e-ISBN 978 0 85721 877 3

First edition 2017

Acknowledgments
Scripture quotations are from the Holy Bible, New International
Version Anglicised. Copyright © 1979, 1984, 2011 Biblica, formerly
International Bible Society. Used by permission of Hodder & Stoughton
Ltd, an Hachette UK company. All rights reserved. "NIV" is a registered
trademark of Biblica. UK trademark number 1448790.

Scripture quotations marked ESV are from The Holy Bible, English
Standard Version® (ESV®) copyright © 2001 by Crossway, a publishing
ministry of Good News Publishers. All rights reserved.

Scripture quotations marked NKJV are from the New King James Version.
Copyright © 1982 by Thomas Nelson, Inc. Used by permission. All right
reserved.

Scripture quotations marked NRSV are from The New Revised Standard
Version of the Bible copyright © 1989 by the Division of Christian
Education of the National Council of Churches in the USA. Used by
permission. All Rights Reserved.

Scripture quotations marked RSV are from The Revised Standard Version
of the Bible copyright © 1946, 1952 and 1971 by the Division of Christian
Education of the National Council of Churches in the USA. Used by
permission. All Rights Reserved.

A catalogue record for this book is available from the British Library

Printed and bound in the UK, January 2018, LH29

Contents

What's All This About?

Today there is a widespread ignorance about real Christianity. Most people think it is finished: the Bible is a bunch of old wives' tales, church is deadly boring, and believers are old-fashioned, narrow-minded, and homophobic. That is one widely held impression. However, to the surprise of many, the Christian faith covers a third of the globe and it is growing faster than ever before, at the rate of about 100,000 new believers worldwide every day. Thousands of young people, adults, and especially students at university are coming to the conviction that God is real, that Jesus brings him to our scene, and that the best decision they could ever make would be to start following him. There are countless new professions of faith each year in the UK alone.

But what then? Ah, there's the rub. There is not much help readily available. New believers are encouraged to read the Bible – but it is a big and difficult book written in three languages over the duration of a thousand years. They are encouraged to go to church, but the experience is often strange and disappointing. They need a starter kit if their profession of faith is to flower into a lifelong commitment. So what we have here is a short introductory course to Christian living for those who have recently professed faith or are seriously considering it. It is written to help folk get started on the road to discipleship (that is, learning from Jesus).

Jesus did not tell his apostles to encourage decisions, but to make disciples. It is not easy to help people to decide for Christ, as anyone knows who has tried it. But sadly a great many of those who have made a profession of faith fall by the wayside and never become true disciples, because they have never been carefully nurtured. And that is tragic.

This short course is designed to help people move from decision to discipleship. It has been used in four continents; it is non-denominational and very flexible. It is very effective for small groups but can also be used with individuals. Intended primarily for genuine enquirers, it is also for those who have recently come to faith. It is not intended for convinced atheists on the one hand or established Christians on the other. To have either in a group tends to disturb the dynamics of those who want to find Christ and grow in him. But it does not hurt to have a few on the fringe or Christians who have lost their way.

So that is what you have in your hand. A six-week course to help you get started and grow in the Christian life.

Guide for Participants

What is the plan?

Most people find evenings the best time to participate on the course, but it can of course run at any time of the day. Let's assume it is the evening. It usually lasts an hour and a half and ends promptly so that people can honour other engagements afterwards.

Each evening begins with refreshments and a chance to chill out for ten minutes or so.

Then there is a short talk on the subject for the night, given by one of the leaders and followed by questions.

Then, to your surprise, you will be asked to repeat and learn by heart a verse of Scripture on the subject of the evening. You will know six such verses, carefully chosen, by the end of the course, and you will be surprised how useful they are and how they come to mind in times of need.

Next the group looks together at a passage from the Bible that is on the subject for the evening, and everyone is invited to contribute their comments and share the bits they like best.

After that there may be a chance for short one-sentence prayers – but fear not, there is no pressure! Before long members like to turn the thought from the Bible passage that has helped them most into a prayer, and perhaps to pray for each other. This encourages members to expect answers to prayer, and share some of these answers week by week as the group meets.

Informal chat and maybe more refreshments ends the evening, but each participant is given a photocopy of the evening's work to take away with them. It will give you a chance to review the topic and go a bit deeper. These weekly handouts are helpful because by the end of six weeks you will have an initial grasp of a number of key elements in Christian discipleship. The topics are as follows:

- Week 1: Introductions and How Can I Start Out as a Christian?

- Week 2: How Can I Be Sure I am a Christian?

- Week 3: How Can I Grown in My Relationship with Jesus?

- Week 4: How Can I Discover Christian Fellowship?

- Week 5: How Can I Experience the Holy Spirit?

- Week 6: How Can I Be Useful to God?

Your notes for each evening are broken down into four sections:

1. A summary of the short talk on the evening's topic.

2. A verse of Scripture on the topic to memorize – along with its reference.

3. A passage of Scripture on the theme for the evening for group Bible study – and some questions to stimulate discussion if needed.

4. Some suggestions for a short time of prayer.

By the way, you will find a good many Bible references in your notes. They are designed partly for the leaders to use if they think appropriate, and partly for members to follow up in their own time. There is, of course, no intention that they should all be looked up then and there!

What are the benefits?

This is not religion. It is not church. Indeed it is best run in a home with food, laughter, and informality. It works well if there are six to eight participants, but it can work with less, and often just a couple of people, one new Christian, and one more experienced Christian can go through it together and gain a lot.

What do you gain? Well I can think of seven benefits straight away.

1. You gain a new perspective. You discover that becoming a disciple is not a matter of solemn faces and cold churches, but learning together with others who are wanting the same thing – to discover who this amazing Jesus is and to get serious about following him.

2. You get the help of experienced leaders who can well remember what it was like to start this Christian life for themselves, the questions they asked, and the mistakes they made. That is really helpful, because no questions are off limits. You can ask and contribute what you want.

3. Another thing you gain is the experience of Christian friendship. You will find a real bond growing between the participants. This is not only a bonus to you all, but is a foretaste of Christian companionship worldwide which is one of the greatest gifts God gives us.

4. You will find that the Bible comes alive. As you read a bit of it and discuss it in the group you will find it addressing you personally, like a letter from some faraway friend whom you love.

5. Prayer becomes a reality. Not reading payers out of a book, but speaking to the Lord as naturally as you would speak to a friend, and before long you will find you are happy to do it out loud among other members of the group.

6. Soon you will find changes in your life. A new joy, a new peace, a desire to do God's will not just your own, a distaste for what you know is wrong, and habits that had chained you getting broken.

7. And I guess you will be wanting others to experience the Jesus who has become real to you, and so you will invite them to somewhere where they can find faith for themselves.

And that's just the start!

So that's what you are in for. I have led scores of groups like this and I find almost everyone loves it and benefits from it. I hope you will.

Guide for Leaders

It is best to have at least two leaders in a group of up to six members; three or four if it is larger. Different leaders offer different gifts and relate to different individuals in the group. They all need to be "people's people" – warm and relational. The overall leader needs to be well-informed on the Bible, on questions that are sure to emerge, and the difficulties new believers are facing. One leader may be better in a teaching role, another at putting members at their ease. All leaders need to know how to help an individual to Christ, how to run a small Bible-study group without dominating it, and how to use the course material. But apart from the main leader you do not need very experienced helpers. Often those who have only been Christians for a year or so are ideal assistants in a course like this. You are going to need more leaders than you might think necessary because of the one-on-one care that will ensue. If a leader has too many participants to look after they will not get the care they need.

General hints

All leaders will have two or three members of the course assigned to them for pastoral care. Aim to have two unhurried sessions with each before this foundation course ends. If they miss a group meeting it is an ideal opportunity for the leader to visit them with the notes of the meeting they have missed and perhaps the offer of a lift to come next time! All leaders will also have a shot at leading (or seconding) one of the inductive Bible studies, and may well be asked to give one of the short talks. The course notes, and especially the talks, are offered as suggestions, not a straitjacket. Feel free to change them according to the needs of the group. There should be a chance for news, questions, and contributions after the short talk each night.

1. The first meeting

This is crucial. Lose them and you have probably lost them for good. Aim to make people feel at ease. In a big group name-tags could be useful for the first couple of weeks. Do not begin the actual meeting until ten minutes after the advertised time, allowing latecomers to arrive and all to have some refreshments and circulate. Announce when the meeting will end – and stick to it. The overall time for the meeting should not exceed ninety minutes.

It is advisable to **start** the first meeting (seated in a circle where you can see everyone) by asking what brings the participants there: "It may seem strange to meet like this in a private home to talk about spiritual things on a Wednesday night. It would be fascinating to find out what brings each of us here." Answer that question for yourself first, bringing in your discovery of Christ. Then go round the group. It helps to have a co-leader sitting on your left who will speak after you. You will thus have provided a couple of models of what you are after. Do not let this get too lengthy (so model your own story concisely), but it is invaluable to see where they are coming from. Welcome each contribution whatever they say, so that they see it is "safe", irrespective of the background they come from and whether they are believers or not. Make clear that these introductions are a "one-off" and will not be repeated, but it will help you as you deal with the participants in the next six weeks, and it will enable them to break the ice and say something about themselves and their beliefs in front of the group.

Then give the **talk**, which one of you leaders will have prepared – usually the main leader for the first two weeks. It need be no more than fifteen minutes long and calls for careful preparation and attractive presentation. Don't just use the suggested material: make it your own. On the first evening you will want to explain exactly what Christianity is and isn't, and make plain the path to responding to Jesus. Don't feel this is premature. They have only come because they are interested, and you only have six sessions! It may be wise to leave by the door some booklets on commitment to Christ. These will quietly vanish as people leave.

You will be under pressure of time for the talk on the first night because of the introductions. The outline talk suggested for the first evening may therefore be too long. So select carefully from it, but make sure that what Jesus has done for us and the means of connecting up with him are made abundantly plain. You may prefer to use a different approach from Revelation 3:20, but clarity is essential. They must understand their need to respond to his gracious initiative.

Open things up for questions, but do not be surprised if on the first night there are not many of them. It is helpful when the questions are over to say, "This response to Jesus really is the heart of the matter. It is so important to get clear about it. So I have left by the door some copies of a little booklet which will enable you to reflect on it in your own time. Do take one as you leave, and read it slowly at your leisure." There are a number of evangelistic booklets available: choose the one you prefer. Michael Ots, *Count Me In!*; Nicky Gumbel, *Why Jesus?*; and Michael Green *Yes!* are among them.

Then slot in **verse learning**, using a touch of humour to introduce such an unexpected thing – laugh and kid them that they are back at Sunday school and then they won't mind. But it is an important element of the evening. They are learning to memorize Scripture and that is invaluable. Repeat the verse (and its reference) twice all together and then without you – and cheerfully warn them you will test them next week!

Now comes the **inductive Bible study** where they discover truth for themselves rather than have you tell them. If you have more than four or five in the group, split it into two, one of them led by another of your leaders. You want everyone to engage, not to have such a large group that some need not say anything. You may decide either to let people split randomly, or organize who goes into which group (and stays there in successive weeks). Only at this point bring out the Bibles – you do not want to frighten the horses by having them on show as they enter the room. They will not have brought a Bible, so you must provide enough for all. Maybe borrow church Bibles. There is great merit in all having the same translation (NIV is probably best) and you can direct them to page numbers rather than the titles of Bible books which they will not know where to find. You may want to run a small book table on the topic for each week, and also have NIV Bibles for sale.

The **end of the meeting** is a good time to offer more refreshments and hand out photocopies of the notes for the evening. See the last pages of the book. You may like to give them a plastic folder in which to store the notes. It is important to do this each week and see that each participant has them so that they can revisit what has been learned, and at the end of six weeks have a basic grasp of the Christian faith. End with a short **prayer**, and conclude the meeting a little before you would really like to. Leave them wanting more! After the meeting the leaders stay on to compare notes on how the evening went, to pray for everyone, and to decide who is going to be pastorally responsible for which member, who will give the talk, teach the verse, and handle the Bible study next week.

Experience shows that there are two main areas where leaders need help: in guiding the inductive Bible study and in doing personal work with individuals under their care. The next two sections will address these issues.

Leading the inductive Bible study

The most important thing to be clear about is that this is not like a talk, with you imparting wisdom! It is exposing people to Scripture so that they find things in it for themselves and share them with the group. Your job is to facilitate that process. Accordingly, here are some things to bear in mind.

1. Ensure that all participants have a Bible with the same translation, and that they are sitting in such a way that you can see everyone's face.

2. Explain where in the Bible the passage for the evening can be found. Suppose it is Acts 9. Say, "The New Testament is the second half of the Bible. First come the four Gospels and then the Acts telling us how the first Christians spread their message." Too simple for some, it will be a lifeline to the embarrassed and the ignorant. Alternatively just give the page number if they all have identical copies.

3. Make sure they all have time to find the passage. Then suggest you read it round in a circle, a verse at a time. This gets people used to the sound of their own voice reading the Bible and helps them to break the sound barrier. You may need to give a few sentences of introductory explanation of what the passage is about, but keep it short.

4. Then give them time to read it again to themselves and choose something that strikes them – a challenge, a command, an encouragement, something they had never seen before, etc. Warn them that we will all be sharing our discovery with one another after two minutes by your watch. That concentrates the mind no end!

5. When the two minutes are up, invite contributions: "Who would like to start?" Someone always will. Make sure they say what verse it is so that everyone can look at it.

6. Try to get them to ask themselves two questions: "What does it mean?" followed by "What could this mean for us today?" You may find mistakes are made in both. If what they say is wildly astray from the meaning of the text you may like to ask, "OK, but what do others think it means?" and then major on the best contribution. If it is unapplied, you can say "Fine, so what is that going to mean in real life for us?"

7. Someone is sure to moan that they wanted to choose that verse too. Say, "Great, this book is inexhaustible. What was it that *you* personally liked about the verse?"

8. You are likely to have the professional talker in your group. Welcome his first and maybe his second contribution, but then say to him gently: "Hang on a moment, Bill. You have given us a couple of very helpful insights. What have other people found?"

9.   You may well have someone who rabbits on down some irrelevant avenue. Enquire gently, "Which verse do you find that in, Jean?" Keep their noses in the text. If they come up with some major issue like predestination or suffering it may be wise to give a very short comment yourself and then encourage the person to chat with you afterwards. Not everyone will want an extended discussion on a topic they are not grabbed by.

10. You are likely to have one or two silent people. Don't frighten them by asking them by name to contribute… for the first couple of weeks. Then you could! But in general, when about to close, say, "Maybe there is someone who hasn't said anything yet who would like to contribute? Great if so."

11. You may find that it all falls prematurely silent. So then you need to prompt discussion by asking questions – there are several in the notes each week, or use your own. But be specific: "There are good things in verse 7. Got any ideas?" And always, in asking questions, avoid those which have a "yes" or "no" answer. "Why?", "How?", or "What does it mean?" usually produce good reflection and answers.

When time is up (say five minutes before the advertised closing time) you might say something like this, but possibly not on the first night: "We have been talking *about* God all evening, and he has been here among us. Why don't we talk *to* him before we go? Tell him what is on your heart or what has helped you this evening. We don't need to kneel down or use formal language. Just take the thought that has most struck you tonight and turn it into a prayer, or thank God for it in your own words. Don't be embarrassed. Christians do pray out loud together, so there is nothing odd about it. And God is not interested in grammar! So let's go for it. I will begin and my fellow leader will close after a brief pause. So do feel free to chip in if you would like to."

Some will probably pray the first time you suggest it, but certainly not all. Don't press them. It will grow on them. You may like to suggest that they just read out the bit of text they like, and then pray very shortly "Thank you for that" or "Please make this true of me." Make sure your own opening prayer is a model – warm, short, and based on the text. Others will probably take the hint. But on the first night it is probably best just for the leader to pray at the end. They have had enough surprises for one night. Think of it – talking about God in a private house on a weekday evening, discovering something of Christian fellowship without even having heard the Word, reading the Bible in the company of people they have never met to get something personal from it, learning a verse by heart. Why, you might think that is enough to prompt a heart attack. But actually it is on the way to transforming the heart!

One-to-one mentoring of each member of the group

Often small groups are less effective than they might be because this one-to-one aspect of ministry is neglected. It is important for the leaders to have two individual sessions with each member during the course. They need to be relaxed and informal chats.

The first chat

It is an enormous privilege to help someone else to find Christ and to grow in him. You need to establish warm, generous relations with the person, and find a setting (ideally over food or drink) that is private enough for you to talk, but also relaxed enough for them to be at ease. Ask them how they are enjoying the course? What have they most liked or disliked? Ask them if they have understood the way to personal relationship with Christ that was explained on the first evening? Have they taken that step of commitment and prayed a prayer of surrender to him – or are they still thinking about it?

They may well tell you that they have indeed done so. If so, rejoice with them. It is the most important decision they have ever made. Show them that they are now in the family, the very household of God (Ephesians 2:19). Show them the contrast between "then" and "now" in, for instance, 1 Peter 2:10. Warn them that there will be problems – we have made a great friend in Jesus but also a great enemy in the devil (James 4:7). Assure them that if they have asked him in, Christ really has entered their lives, because he promised he would (Revelation 3:20; John 6:37, and so on). Feelings will come and go: the new believer needs to rely on the promise of the One who cannot lie, and gradually the fruit of the new life will appear (Galatians 5:22ff.). It would help them if you could show them one verse of Scripture to take away: John 6:37 is no bad choice.

But they may well tell you they have not yet taken that step. If so, your job is gently to discover why.

A good diagnostic question might be: "Is that because of something you don't understand, or maybe because of something you feel you can't face?" If it is something they do not understand, then you need to go through God's plan of salvation with them again. Or it may be a problem like suffering or other faiths which is holding them back. This will need patient listening and loving care.

But if it is something they can't face up to or are unwilling to do, that is because, in all probability, they feel the cost is too great. They feel they may lose their friends. Christ might diminish their lives and make them seem over-religious. Or perhaps the whole idea of letting control go to Jesus is too frightening. You need to be very understanding, but to respond to whatever the obstacle is. Of course they may lose friends, but such will be pretty poor friends. The better ones may laugh at them to begin with but will soon respect them and perhaps begin to start investigating for themselves. You need to make them see that Christ will not narrow or diminish their lives. Did he not promise, "I have come that they may have life, and have it to the full" (John 10:10)? After all, we are not called to be religious in the dull, conventional sense. We are offered friendship with the most wonderful person who has ever lived. So gently handle the presenting objections, but be wary of pressing a person for a decision. That is the Holy Spirit's job, not ours. Our job is to paint the attractiveness of life with Jesus, and issue his invitation.

If you sense that they are responsive, you might ask, "Would you rather make your response to Jesus on your own, or with me?" Usually they go for the latter, since they have come to trust you on such issues by now. But if they choose to make their response on their own, encourage them to come and tell you once they have done so. That will seal it in their own minds, and will enable you to give them encouragement. If they prefer to do it with you, pray out loud that they may have the courage to take the plunge, and then say "OK, take your time, and then in your own words ask Jesus to come and share your life." They may well ask you if that means they have to pray aloud, which they have probably never done. I tend to say, "No, praying aloud is not part of the deal. The Lord can hear you just as well if you pray silently in your heart. But I can't – and I thought you wanted me to be in on it! Anyhow, Christians do pray aloud together, and it might be a good idea to break the sound barrier and begin as you mean to go on." You will find that after an agonizing delay they generally pour out their heart in prayer, however doubtful about it they may have been beforehand. Sometimes, however, it is very brief and transactional. That does not matter. It is the will you are after, not the emotions. Emotion may or may not accompany the act of surrender to Christ. In any case rejoice with them, and perhaps suggest they make another prayer, thanking Christ for coming to them. They may not feel he has; so point them to the promise he has made and cannot break: "Did you ask him in? Right, in that case he has come in because he promised to do so. Meanwhile it would be grateful, would it not, to give him a big thank you?"

The joy of leading someone to the feet of Jesus is enormous. There is nothing to match it!

The second chat

This will take place towards the end of the course, by which time you will have got to know the members of your group fairly well. You will want to discover if there are any major problems they are encountering. You will want to find out if they are beginning to have a regular devotional life, and may need to get them Bible-reading notes from Scripture Union or the Bible Reading Fellowship, both of which are helpful and offer a range of notes for different ages and levels of understanding. Equally, you will want to see if your friend is starting to pray, and ask them, perhaps, for some example of answers to their prayers. It is important to check that they are introduced to a lively Bible-teaching church, and you will want to help them think ahead to what smaller fellowship, such as a home group, they should join once the foundation course is over, and what service for Christ they are beginning to consider. To engage in some form of ministry for Christ is, of course, one of the great ways to grow in the Christian life.

Postscript

Well, after six weeks your role as leader or co-leader of this little group will have ended, but you will still have responsibility to see that each of the group whom you are personally looking after is helped to settle into a new fellowship. In student life this will be the Christian Union. In parish life it will be a home group of the local church. You will have had your second personal chat with them, and will have a good idea of where they are headed. It would be helpful to see that they have got some Bible-reading notes, and are beginning to form a prayer list. It is ideal if a newish believer can occasionally read a bit of the Bible with a more mature Christian friend, and you may be able to facilitate that. You have had a big hand in their formation, so continue to pray for them, be available to help them if they ask for it, and call them up or give them a meal from time to time to see how they are doing. Paul had a particular love for the Christians at Corinth, difficult though some of them were. He reminds them that though they had many teachers in Christ, they do not have many fathers, and reminds them that in Christ Jesus he had become their father (1 Corinthians 4:15). You will have become the spiritual father or mother of some of those in your group, and a great help to others. Show them the same affection that Paul did. "I urge you to imitate me," he says. As for you, you are unlikely to have a more exciting and significant six weeks of ministry this year than in leading a foundation course! Thank God for the privilege.

Week 1

How Can I Start Out as a Christian?

The talk

The word "Christian" is so broad nowadays that it is almost meaningless. Is it being brought up in a Christian home? Doing good and helping others? Being baptized and confirmed? Believing in God? Christianity may embrace all four. But it is possible to tick all those boxes and still not be a Christian. For Christianity is not primarily a matter of churchgoing – all sorts of reasons lead people to church. It is not a matter of ceremonies – there are countless baptized unbelievers around. It is not a matter of creeds – a well-educated parrot can squawk the creed. It is not a matter of conduct – many Muslims and atheists lead good lives but are not Christians. No, real Christianity is all about Christ. That's why it is called *Christ*ianity. It's all about him.

Did he ever live, or is it all a fairy tale?

Yes, he was a real historical figure. Not only is all history divided into BC and AD, what came before and after Christ, but secular writers of the period like the Roman historian Tacitus (*Annals* 15.44) and the Jewish historian Josephus (*Antiquities* 18.3) attest his birth, some of his teaching, his execution by the Romans, the rumour of his resurrection, and the start of the church.

Who was this remarkable figure?

There is a hint in the names given him at his birth: "Emmanuel" ("God is with us") and "Jesus" ("God to the rescue"). Truly human, a carpenter by trade, he convinced those who knew him that he was more than human. His sheer authority, his teaching, his fulfilment of many prophecies uttered centuries earlier, his matchless character and love for all, his claims (to forgive sins, to accept worship, to be one with God the Father, to be the "resurrection and the life") are the ravings of a lunatic if they are not true. Can anyone in their right mind dismiss

Jesus as a lunatic? And those claims of his were backed by a matchless life and miracles of healing. But it was his sacrificial death and well-attested resurrection that finally persuaded these monotheistic Jewish followers of his that the unthinkable had happened, and God had indeed come among his people on earth.

Why did he come?

He came because we all misuse our God-given free will and refuse to love and obey the Creator who has given us life. We humans are determined to go our own way. In the language of the Bible we have all sinned. And sin, or rebellion against God, is serious. It spoils lives, imposes a bondage; it separates from God, and it is fatal if not dealt with. You may feel you are not so bad, and better than most. But that's not the point. None of us has lived up to our own standards, let alone God's perfect standard, revealed to us in the life of Jesus. We sin when we can't be bothered with God or with other people and say, "I am my own boss. It's my life and I shall do what I like with it." How true of Isaiah to observe, "All we like sheep have gone astray; we have turned every one to his own way" (RSV, Isaiah 53:6). That is sin, and it cuts us off from God.

God has to repudiate that attitude. He has to show that it is wrong. We should be banished from his holy presence. But the wonderful news Jesus brings is that, instead of taking it out on us, God has burdened himself with our wrongdoings. He has taken personal responsibility for our sins. He has himself carried the foul load of human wickedness so that we should never have to bear it. That is the central meaning of the cross.

And just before he died Jesus cried, "It is finished." This was the cry not of despair but of victory. The job of reconciling man to God was complete. The bridge back to the heavenly Father was finished.

But that was not the end of him. Jesus rose from the grip of death. Death could not hold down the Lord of life. The evidence for this amazing thing is powerful, and we might discuss it later. But that has been the claim of his followers from the start. It is what got the church going in the first place. Jesus died to deal with the blockage our sin creates – the blockage that cuts us off from God. And he rose from the dead to demonstrate the completion of his rescue, and to show us the new quality of life beyond death that awaits his followers. More, Jesus was raised from the dead so that he could be released from the confines of a single body and be available to share the lives of all who would put their trust in him. It is only when we welcome him into our lives that we can truly call ourselves Christians.

But how do I get in touch?

The answer is simple, so simple that many people miss it. It is as basic as ABCD.

A.   **There is something to admit**

We have to admit that we are out of touch with God, and that the fault lies with us. We have the "human disease" of sin, which consists of breaking God's law, coming short of his standards, and rejecting his love and authority over us. The results of this disease are serious. We are estranged from God (Isaiah 59:1, 2; Ephesians 2:1) and enslaved to self-centredness (John 8:34). The disease is fatal if not dealt with (Romans 6:23). In order to start a relationship with Jesus we need to admit this and be willing for a change. Nothing we do can remedy the situation. Even if we could live a perfect life from now on that would not atone for the past. "None is righteous, no, not one" (RSV, Romans 3:10) and a holy God cannot have defilement in his presence.

B.   **There is something to believe**

We need to believe that Jesus has done all that is necessary to restore relations with God, through his birth, his death on the cross, and his risen life. His birth shows how much God cares about us in coming in person to find us. His death takes responsibility for our misdoings (1 Peter 3:18), and the fact he rose from the dead means he is alive, available, and able to free us from our bondage to selfishness (John 8:36).

C. There is something to consider

And that is the cost of discipleship. Although the entrance fee to the Christian life is nothing at all, the annual subscription is all we have got. Nobody can serve two masters: we cannot serve the true God and also society's god of materialism (Matthew 6:24). Following Jesus is tough and includes being willing to go public, where appropriate, about our allegiance (Romans 10:9, 10), and getting involved in Christian fellowship (Hebrews 10:25). There is bound to be opposition, as well.

D. There is something to do

We need to receive the gift that is Jesus Christ. All God's other gifts are wrapped up in him (Ephesians 1:3). There are many ways in which the New Testament describes this clinching of the deal – adoption, access, entering into Christ, and so forth. But perhaps the clearest comes in Revelation 3:20: "Here I am! I stand at the door and knock. If anyone hears my voice and opens the door, I will come in." Christ is excluded from our lives until we invite him in. He is love, and will not force himself on us. We need to ask him in. It is a superb illustration, and yet it is more than an illustration, because when a person opens up to Christ, his unseen but real Holy Spirit does come in. Something happens. We are not the same as we were before. The Spirit of Christ has taken up residence.

There are actually three sides to becoming a Christian. Repentance and faith is the personal side. Baptism is the public side. Receiving the Holy Spirit is the divine side. You are only truly a Christian when you have welcomed the Holy Spirit into your life (Romans 8:9). And that is possible for every one of us. Don't miss it!

Verse of Scripture to Learn

There is real value in learning to internalize a verse of Scripture. On this first night Revelation 3:20 is the obvious choice:

"HERE I AM! I STAND AT THE DOOR AND

KNOCK. IF ANYONE HEARS MY VOICE AND

OPENS THE DOOR, I WILL COME IN."

So we say it a couple of times together – with its reference.

Bible study: Zacchaeus the Tax Collector

Luke 19:1–10. This story from the Gospels continues the theme that the heart of Christianity is relationship with Jesus Christ. The story of Saul's conversion (Acts 9:1–19) would be an alternative, as would Jesus' discussion with Nicodemus on the new birth (John 3:1–16). But the story of Zacchaeus is perhaps the clearest and most arresting. So with open Bibles, a word of introduction, and a short prayer for understanding we read the passage round the group, then reflect on it quietly before sharing what strikes us most.

Stimulating questions:

1. Why do you think Zacchaeus felt the need to meet Jesus? Why do we?

2. Why did Jesus bother about the disreputable Zacchaeus?

3. Did Zacchaeus have to smarten up his life before Jesus would enter his home?

4. What does Jesus bring when he comes into someone's life?

5. What difference did Jesus' visit make to Zacchaeus?

Session Notes

Session Notes

Week 2

How Can I Be Sure I Am a Christian?

There may well be some questions arising from last week, or maybe someone has had a prayer answered during the week. It is amazing how quickly some very new believers find their tentative prayers wonderfully answered. And as one or two share, it is an enormous encouragement to others.

The talk

1 John 5:9–15. When we get linked up with Jesus (receive him, come to him, come to know him – it does not matter which image we use, and the Bible uses them all) we need to be clear where we stand. Can we really be sure of him? Is the relationship permanent? It is common to have doubts, especially early on in the Christian life. And it is important to deal with these doubts. You cannot build a solid house on shifting foundations, nor can you build a confident Christian life if you are unsure whether you belong to Christ or not.

Scripture anticipates, and answers the immediate questions which usually crowd in:

- Can I be sure I am accepted? Yes (John 6:37).

- Will God hold my past failures against me? He will not (Romans 8:1).

- When I fail, do I lose my place in the family? No, but I need to come back and repent (1 John 1:9).

- Can I keep it up? Not by myself, but Jesus can keep me up! (2 Corinthians 12:9).

- How can I overcome my temptations? (1 Corinthians 10:13).

It is so important for us to know where we stand, that the whole Trinity has got involved. The first letter of John tells us all about it. We hear about:

The Word of God the Father

In 1 John 5:10–12 the writer makes a powerful point. If we believe human testimony it stands to reason that we should believe God's testimony. If not, we are charging God with lying, which is ridiculous: "And this is the testimony: that God has given us eternal life, and this life is [all wrapped up] in His Son. He who has the Son has life; he who does not have the Son of God does not have life" (NKJV, verses 11–12). It makes sense, doesn't it? How does an applicant know they have got the job? When a contract signed by the boss is delivered to them. How does the hopeful sixth-former know they have been accepted at their chosen university? When they get a letter from the competent authority telling them that they have secured a place. Whether they feel they deserve it or not is irrelevant. They are accepted! God's word of acceptance is no less reliable.

The work of God the Son

John is very clear that the work of Christ on the cross cancels out our sins, and makes access to God eminently possible. We see it in 2:2, "He is the atoning sacrifice for our sins, and not for ours only but also for the sins of the whole world" (RSV). Again in 4:10: "This is love, not that we loved God but that he loved us and sent his Son as an atoning sacrifice for our sins". This is an important point to stress, because the new believer can fall into deep depression when they find their habitual failures have not disappeared yet. The tempter will do his best to make them despair and give up. They need to know that payment has been made – the job has been done once and for all.

I recall buying a book years ago and later having a bill sent to me for it. For once I had kept the receipt. So I went and presented it, and told them firmly the bill had been paid. They apologized profusely. The new believer needs to see that Jesus has made a sacrifice that has lasting effectiveness. The bill, so to speak, has been paid. It will never be presented again.

The witness of God the Holy Spirit

This little letter of 1 John is full of confidence. "We know" comes time after time. John is very concerned that Christians should know that they belong. And the Holy Spirit, once he is welcomed into our lives, progressively makes himself known. As John puts it (3:24): "this is how we know that he lives in us: We know it by the Spirit he gave us". Very well, just what does the Spirit grow in the garden of our lives once he has been planted there? Gradually we shall find clear marks of his presence. They will not all come at once, nor in any special order, but they *will* come. And it will all be wonderfully new. John outlines what we may expect:

- a new desire to please God (2:5) which we certainly did not have before

- a new assurance of pardon when we fail and come humbly back to him (1:9; 2:1–2)

- a new willingness to face opposition for our convictions (3:13)

- a new delight in the company of fellow Christians (3:14) whom we might have scorned before

- a new generosity of spirit to people in need (3:17)

- a new experience of victory over temptation (4:4; 5:4)

- a new discovery of prayer being answered (3:22; 5:14)

- a new understanding and set of priorities (5:20, 21).

The point John is making is that the whole Trinity is concerned to assure us that once we have entrusted ourselves to Christ we are permanently welcome in the Father's house. We are meant to know we belong. Not think, or hope, but be fully assured: "I write these things to you who believe on the name of the Son of God that you may know that you have [*not will have or may have*] eternal life" (ESV, 5:13).

Verse of Scripture to Learn

"HE WHO HAS THE SON HAS LIFE;

HE WHO DOES NOT HAVE THE SON

OF GOD DOES NOT HAVE LIFE."

(NKJV, 1 JOHN 5:12)

Without Jesus we may have much else, but we have no part in the life of the age to come. It is a wonderfully encouraging verse to learn. If we have said, "Yes" to Jesus and welcomed him into our lives, then we have the first instalment of everlasting life. And it is all due to God's generosity.

Bible study: Saul's conversion

Acts 9:1–22 tells the story of the conversion of Saul of Tarsus. Much of his story is unique, but much applies to every person who discovers Jesus for himself. Questions to tease out might include the following:

1. Saul of Tarsus (later known as Paul) was intelligent, religious, virtuous, enthusiastic, and sincere. Surely such a man needs no conversion, then or now?

2. Later on in his life, Paul called his conversion "an example" (1 Timothy 1:16). In what ways is this true?

3. Was there any "Ananias" to help you in your discovery of Jesus?

4. What differences began to be seen in Saul's life that convinced him and others that the change was real?

Alternatively we could choose Romans 8:8–17. This is a long chapter, full of good things, about the Holy Spirit's work in us. You could look at part of it now in verses 8–17.

1. In verses 9, 15, and 16 the apostle describes our relationship with God in two different ways. What are these two images? Which says more to you?

2. Examine verses 10–14 and find some of the differences between a person who is linked to Christ and one who is not.

3. Can we expect the Christian life to be easy? See verse 17. How can this verse encourage us in hard times?

4. Reflect on verses 15, 26, and 27. What do these verses teach us about prayer?

Prayer time

God has no dumb children! He wants us to talk to him as naturally as we talk to one another. In family life, all the members usually join in the conversation together. It is meant to be like that in God's family. Many of us will not have prayed out loud before. Praying silently is just as effective as praying out loud, but if we pray aloud, it helps us to concentrate our own prayers and it enables others to say "Amen" in agreement. Let's choose one thing we have learned this evening, or one verse that particularly struck us. In a short sentence let's thank the Lord for it or pray that it may become true for us.

Many also find it helpful to pray out loud when they are on their own. Not only does it help us to concentrate, but it gets us used to putting our prayers into words and hearing ourselves pray.

Session Notes

Session Notes

Week 3

How Can I Grow in My Relationship With Jesus?

The talk

When we come to Jesus, it is not the end of the business, but the beginning: the beginning of a new life which needs to be developed. Indeed, one of the pictures the New Testament gives is that of new birth (John 3:5, 7). It is as though we are born into a new life, and like our physical life it needs developing. We would be shocked if we came across somebody who had never grown. Sadly there are Christians like that. We look at personal growth this week, and next week at growing within the Christian family.

Two of the great ways of developing our personal relationship with Jesus are by Bible reading on a regular basis, and prayer. That is very similar to the way you would develop a relationship with someone you care about but cannot see. You would use a letter or an email, the phone or Skype. It is much the same with the Lord. We cannot see him, but the Bible is his letter to us. Prayer is talking to and listening to him.

The Bible

What is the Bible?

It is not so much a book as a library. It contains sixty-six books written by some forty authors in three languages over more than 1,000 years. You will find many different literary genres and styles here – poetry, prose, history, story, biography, ethical instruction, letters, and much more. But behind the human authors, God was inspiring their message (2 Timothy 3:14–17; 2 Peter 1:21). It is not primarily a history book, a textbook, or a handbook of ethics, though it contains all three. It is essentially a collection of "letters from heaven" as St Augustine put it, through which God wants to speak to us and build us up. Its main theme is "salvation" – God's intervention into our world to rescue us from our self-centredness and rebellion. Progressively it shows us what God is like, and how to relate to him. The centrepiece of the Bible is Jesus. The Old Testament points forward to him, the Gospels show him in all his winsomeness, and the rest of the New Testament looks back to him and draws out the implications of his coming.

Why read it?

See what it can do for us. It is described as a mirror (James 1:22–25) to show us what we are like. It is a sword to use in temptation (Ephesians 6:17). It is a hammer to break down our obstinacy (Jeremiah 23:29). It is described as sweet honey and nourishing milk for spiritual babes, and strong meat for mature believers (Ezekiel 3:3; 1 Peter 2:2; and Hebrews 5:12–14). It can cleanse us, guide us, and give us wisdom (Psalm 119:9, 165). We can find guidance and peace in its pages (Psalms 119:105; Proverbs 4:4–6). It is a prime way of keeping in touch with the Lord (John 15:7). There are a lot of good reasons there!

How do we read it?

Get a modern version of the Bible you can treasure: the NIV is probably the most accurate, and the Good News Bible a brilliant paraphrase. Get a scheme for regular daily reading, and it helps to get some useful notes such as those of Scripture Union, Bible Reading Fellowship or *Every Day with Jesus* by Selwyn Hughes. Ask yourself a) What did this mean to the original recipients? b) How does this apply to me? Then turn what you found into prayer and thanksgiving.

Wandering thoughts

How are we to handle these? Turn those wandering thoughts into a short prayer, and then return to what you were reading previously. If there are things you want to remember to do, jot them down on your phone or in a little notebook.

Prayer

There is a world of difference between knowing about a person and actually knowing him. It is in prayer that we get to know God, discover something of his mind and join in his purposes. In prayer we receive much more than we give, but there are some aspects of prayer that we may find helpful:

- Praise – appreciating and enjoying him for who he is (Psalm 96:7–8).

- Confession – getting rid of blotches on the page (Psalm 32:3–5).

- Meditation – reflecting on our Scripture passage (Psalm 119:48).

- Thanks – for his gifts, his rescue, and his answers to prayer (Psalm 103:1–5).

- Requests – for others and for our own lives (Matthew 7:7; 1 Thessalonians 5:25).

- Listening – quietly sensing there is something God wants to say to us (Romans 8:26).

- Offering – ourselves for his service (Romans 12:1–2).

Always remember that prayer is not twisting God's ear for what we want, but seeking to ally ourselves to his purposes.

Learning to pray

Though prayer is as natural as speech, like speech it has to be learned.

We learn by doing it, primarily by setting a regular time for it daily (see a busy man's example in Daniel 6:10). Pray alone (Mark 1:35) and with others (Matthew 18:20). Learn, too, to pray brief "arrow" prayers as need arises (Nehemiah 2:4–5 and Matthew 14:30).

We learn from Jesus, starting with his great pattern prayer (Luke 11:1–13) and going on to his meditation in John 17.

We learn, too, from the Holy Spirit who is given to help us in our prayers (Romans 8:15–16 and 26–27).

Unanswered prayer

We feel let down when this happens, but maybe we should just ask ourselves some questions. Do we actually pray (James 4:2)? And mean it (Matthew 7:7)? Are our goals selfish (James 4:3)? Is there unconfessed sin in the way (James 4:8)? Do we persevere in prayer (Luke 18:1–8)? Are we seeking our own will rather than God's (Mark 14:36)? Answers do not always come in the form we expect or at the time we demand. We may sometimes be meant to answer our own prayers (Matthew 14:15–16). The answer may be God's "no" or "wait". And perhaps he wants to encourage us to love him for himself, not for something we can get from him!

Verse of Scripture to learn

"YOUR WORD IS A LAMP FOR MY

FEET, A LIGHT ON MY PATH."

(PSALM 119:105)

Bible study: Thanksgiving and prayer

Read Colossians 1:3–24, one of the many examples of the way Paul prayed for Christians.

1. What are the main things for which Paul thanks God in the lives of these people he had never met?

2. Why is thanksgiving such an important part of prayer?

3. Paul is not slow to ask God for things in prayer. What sort of things? And how should we pray for our friends?

4. Paul prays that they may know God's power; what sort of things is that power to do?

5. What are the main marks of Christian discipleship in this passage?

An alternative passage, focusing more on the Bible itself, could be Acts 8:26–40.

1. What was the traveller doing as he rode along? Why did he need help?

2. How exactly did Philip help him? What might be the modern equivalent of the help Philip offered?

3. What effect should a fresh understanding of the Bible have on us as we expose ourselves to it?

4. Where does the Holy Spirit come into all this?

Prayer time

Take a verse or a phrase from the chosen passage and turn it into a prayer, first for yourself and then for a friend. Revisit some of the things about the Bible or prayer that struck you this evening, and wrap your prayers around them.

Session Notes

Session Notes

Session Notes

Week 4

How Can I Discover Christian Fellowship?

The talk

Christian living is not an isolated affair, but a matter of belonging with others in God's countercultural society, the church.

The nature of the church

The church has a bad image in many people's eyes but in reality it is exciting. Here are some of the descriptions the Bible gives of the church. It is not a building, or a hierarchy, or even an organization. It is the family of God (Galatians 4:4–7), the bride of Christ (2 Corinthians 11:1–3; Revelation 21:2–8), the temple of the Spirit (Ephesians 2:19–22). It is the colony of heaven (Philippians 3:20), the body of Christ (Ephesians 4:15–16), and the army of God (Ephesians 6:12–20).

The job of the church

The Bible is equally clear as to what the church's functions are. The three main ones are worship of God, fellowship with one another, and witness and service to society. Significantly some verses such as 1 Peter 2:1–12 interweave all three.

The unity of the church

Jesus prayed for his followers to be united (John 17:20–21) and they managed it, more or less, in the early days. In due course, however, human frailty and particular emphases led to the creation of denominations. But God hates division in his people. Despite all appearances there is a God-given unity among all true Christians (Ephesians 4:4–6). We must seek to preserve and regain that unity.

The church – a classless society

The New Testament knows nothing of a clergy–laity division. It knows nothing about denominations. And it is very clear that nominal membership is not enough. The church is a one-class society transcending all barriers of sex, age, colour, class, and nationality (Galatians 3:28; Ephesians 2:14–18). It knows no different status among Christians, only differing functions (Ephesians 4:11, 12). Love is the bond that should unite us all.

The church's paradoxical character

The church is both universal (Matthew 16:18) and local (for example, Colossians 1:2). It is invisible but has visible manifestations. Repentance and faith is the gateway into God's invisible church (1 Peter 2:4) and baptism is the mark of members of the visible church. However, outward belonging does not guarantee inner commitment, but should accompany it. One of the church's problems is the large number who have the outward mark of baptism but no inner union with Christ.

The church's sacraments

Jesus left two physical marks for his new community. One was baptism, the unrepeatable entry rite (Matthew 28:19), and the other was the regular family meal, the Holy Communion, which Jesus gave us in memory of his death, as a means of drawing on his living support, and as a foretaste of heaven (1 Corinthians 11:23–26). If you have not been baptized you should request it. Then you will be able to join in the family meal. It is a great way to grow in the Christian life.

Informal fellowship

Christians get together not only in Sunday worship, but also informally in homes, pubs, and restaurants. It is natural for birds of a feather to flock together, and so it is for believers to enjoy each other's company in play, laughter, discussion, meals, and prayer.

Verse of Scripture to Learn

"NOW YOU ARE THE BODY OF

CHRIST, AND EACH ONE OF YOU

IS A PART OF IT."

1 CORINTHIANS 12:27

Bible study: Sacrifice and service

The Bible passage for study tonight is Romans 12:1–13.

1. What does true worship involve?

2. The church is Christ's body on earth. What implications flow from that? Do you see them in your local church?

3. If "each member belongs to all the others" (verse 5) what does this mean for our relationships?

4   According to Paul we all have different gifts and abilities. What main gifts does each of you think you have? What do others in the group think you have? How are your gifts being used for the common good in your church or college group?

5. See what this passage has to say about the practical fruits that flow from wholehearted surrender to Jesus. Is anything holding you back from presenting your body "as a living sacrifice"?

Prayer time

Get into pairs. Pray over the use of each other's gifts. Then think of one thing you would like to see happen in your church or student group. Pray for it, and commit to do so during the coming week.

Session Notes

Session Notes

Session Notes

Week 5

How Can I Experience the Holy Spirit?

The talk

The Holy Spirit was not initiated by Jesus. He is the eternal life of God in the world of men and women. He was there at the beginning (Genesis 1:2–3; 2:7). In the Old Testament he was bestowed on special people for special tasks: in particular the prophets, priests, and kings of Israel were gifted with the Spirit. But they looked for the coming of the Messiah when the Spirit would be widely available (Ezekiel 36:25–27; Jeremiah 31:31–34; Isaiah 11:1; Joel 2:28–32). Jesus was the person uniquely filled with the Holy Spirit (John 1:32; 7:37–39). He promised that after his death the Spirit, his "other self", would come and live within the lives of believers (John 14:15–18; 16:7–15). That is just what happened at Pentecost (Acts 2). Since then, in contrast to Old Testament days, the Spirit is for all believers, not some. He is not fitful but remains with us, unwithdrawn. He is no longer impersonal, but marked with the character of Jesus.

The fruit of the Spirit

The Holy Spirit enters our lives at conversion (Galatians 4:6). He then sets to work getting lovely fruit to grow in the garden of our lives: love, joy, peace, and so forth (Galatians 5:22–24). As we, the branches, stay in Christ the vine, the sap of God's Spirit slowly but surely produces fruit (John 15:1–15). We cannot create these fruits of character: that is the Spirit's work. But, alas, we can prevent them growing if we grieve or quench the Holy Spirit (Ephesians 4:30; 1 Thessalonians 5:10).

The gifts of the Spirit

The Holy Spirit is a great giver. He gave inspiration to the Scriptures (2 Timothy 3:16; 2 Peter 1:21), incarnation to Jesus (Luke 1:35; 4:14), and new life to sinners (Romans 6:23; Ezekiel 37:1–14). He also equips the people of God to live an approximation of the life of heaven here on earth. There are important examples of his gifts in 1 Corinthians 12:4–13 and Romans 12:3–13, some of which fell into disuse but are being recovered today. His supreme aim is to make us like Christ (2 Corinthians 3:18).

The power of the Spirit in temptation

One of the great functions of the Holy Spirit in the believer is to give power to overcome temptation. Temptation is a universal experience and it increases after we become Christians – naturally, because we have changed sides. Temptation comes through "the world" (the society which leaves God out – 1 John 2:15, 16), "the flesh" (our own fallen nature, Romans 7:21–23), and "the devil" (the anti-God force of evil, 1 Thessalonians 3:5).

The devil is no figure of fun but awesomely real; one of God's angelic creatures who rebelled against God and wants to wreck all that is good in God's world. Jesus clearly believed in him (Matthew 4:1–11) and our experience points the same way (1 Peter 5:8, 9).

Genesis 3 shows him at work. He is carefully disguised as a serpent, and attacks through the body (twisting our proper desires, verse 6), the mind (casting doubt on God's goodness, verse 1), his word (verse 1), and wrongful ambition (the itch to be top dog, verses 3–5). All of these attacks are designed to reach the will (verse 6). Only when we yield to temptation does it turn into sin.

The results of yielding to temptation stand out clearly in this story. It makes us feel guilty (verses 7, 9, 10). It hurts other people (verse 6). It makes God seem unreal and unwelcome (verses 8, 9). It produces fear and moral cowardice (verses 10–12), and it brings God's judgment (verses 14, 15).

Jesus was tempted more than any of us but never gave way to it (Hebrews 4:15). Because he won the major war, he can help us with our smaller battles too (Hebrews 2:18). He does so through the power of his Holy Spirit who lives in us (Romans 8:11, 13; Galatians 5:16) and as we turn to the Lord at the approach of temptation, he progressively turns our defeats into victories.

Victory secrets

It is worth remembering that in our temptations there is always a way through – if we will take it (1 Corinthians 10:13). We must call quickly on the power of the Spirit when temptation strikes. And we must not self-destruct by playing with temptations. Let's not flirt with "the world" – society, films, magazines, talk, the web, and ambitions which dull our love for Christ. Let's not spare "the flesh" – that selfish "me" needs to be kept on the cross daily so that the Spirit can flourish in us (Galatians 2:20; Romans 8:13). And let's not compromise with "the devil". Resist him (James 4:7; 1 Peter 5:9), and keep clear of his favourite area, the occult (Acts 19:18–20). A half-hearted Christian life not only lets Jesus down before others; it is also miserable for us!

Verse of Scripture to learn

"I CAN DO ALL THINGS THROUGH

HIM WHO STRENGTHENS ME."

NRSV, PHILIPPIANS 4:13

Bible study: Spiritual gifts

The Bible passage for study tonight is 1 Corinthians 12:1–13.

1. How does verse 3 link Jesus with the Holy Spirit?

2. What do you learn from the variety of gifts and their unified source?

3. What do verses 8–10 teach about the kind of ministries we should be exercising in our churches?

4. What is meant by being "given the one Spirit to drink"? See John 7:37–39.

5. Does this passage give any support to the idea that there are two kinds of Christians – ordinary and "Spirit-filled"?

6. Will you ask the Spirit to fill you and equip you for service with whatever gifts he sees to be needed? "Ask and you will receive, and your joy will be complete" (John 16:24).

An alternative passage might be Genesis 3. Whatever the literary genre, it gives a great insight into temptation.

1. What was the prime cause of mankind's fall from grace?

2. What was the devil's supreme aim?

3. Why did he succeed?

4. What did the man and the woman hope to gain?

5. What were the consequences of yielding to temptation?

6. What hint is there of God's ultimate victory?

Prayer time

Prayer should be flowing freely by now. But it might be good for all the members of the group to write down two main things they want the Spirit to do in them. If they feel free to do so, they can share them with the group, and then all pray for one another.

And hey! – next week is the final meeting of our group. Let's have a bring-and-share supper to celebrate, as we prepare to go our different ways.

Session Notes

Session Notes

Session Notes

Week 6

How Can I Be Useful to God?

The talk

There are perhaps two main ways in which we can show our gratitude to God.

Witness

We do not join the army, the police, or a sports team, without putting on the uniform. We want to make it crystal clear that we belong. And it is the same with the Christian life. Some people are ashamed to admit they are Christians, and tend to deny their allegiance if they are in the company of unbelievers. Some people keep a low profile and hope nobody will ask! Both are unworthy.

It is noteworthy that on the day of Pentecost Peter gave the sermon but all the disciples gave their testimony: "God has raised this Jesus to life, and we are all witnesses of it" (Acts 2:32). Witness became a major theme in New Testament times. All Christians are called to be unembarrassed about their love for Christ. Romans 10:9–10 makes it very clear that public confession of Christ is as important as private commitment to him. It is only as we "believe in [our] heart" and "confess with [our] mouth" that we shall be saved. Secret disciples are a liability to the Christian cause.

In many countries like Indonesia, and almost all the Muslim world, Christians are likely to be killed simply for belonging to Jesus. Yet we in the West hardly dare mention the name of Jesus outside a church service. The Lord calls us to something more courageous than this. The New Testament is adamant that we are all called to be witnesses to Jesus. Not preachers – that is the calling for some. But all are called to be witnesses. A witness does not preach. He or she simply relates their experience. And Christians are called to do just that. We must all be able to say, when appropriate, "I have found Jesus has made a power of difference to me." The good thing is that nobody can argue with your experience, so it need not be frightening! The church needs fewer indifferent preachers and more confident witnesses. Interestingly, in the New Testament, the word "witness" always indicates witness to Jesus and the fact that he is alive. It is well to keep that emphasis and not get too involved in the subjective aspects of our own experience. However we go about it, like Paul, every believer can say, "I am not ashamed of the gospel, because it is the power of God that brings salvation to everyone who believes" (Romans 1:16). After all, how can people know the reality of Jesus unless those who know him are prepared to say so? Why don't we try that now? Let's go round the group and everyone can say whether or not they have yet given their lives to Christ, and if so what difference he has made. It should be easy here since we all know each other quite well. Treat it as a dummy run for harder occasions! Who's going to kick off?

Service

The whole ministry of Jesus was one of service. He came not to be served but to serve (Mark 10:45). Service not status was the leadership pattern that Jesus adopted. And he asked his followers to do the same (John 13:12–17). Every Christian is a minister or servant of Christ. It is impossible to be a Christian without having some ministry to do for Jesus. Don't restrict the name "minister" to missionaries and pastors. It includes all of us.

There are three main words for "servant" or "minister" in the Greek of the New Testament. All three apply to all Christians.

The slave

The first is *doulos*, slave (1 Peter 2:16; Revelation 1:1). It describes the total surrender of every part of our lives – home, work, love life, ambitions, and the lot, to Jesus who is also called a *doulos* and gave up everything for us. Ponder Romans 12:1–2 and 1 Corinthians 6:19–20. In ancient society the slave had no rights, no money, and was not allowed to marry. He was totally at the disposal of his master. The New Testament deliberately and shockingly chose this word "slave" to describe one aspect of their relation to Jesus. How does it fit you?

The worship leader

The second word, *leitourgos*, means worship leader. We get our word liturgy from it. It speaks of our worship (Acts 13:2). It too is a word that belongs to all Christians. Worship is a big word. It includes our giving (2 Corinthians 9:12), our faith (Philippians 2:7), doing our job properly (Romans 13:6), even evangelism (Romans 15:16). We might usefully ask ourselves how important worship is to us. What does it cost us? Does it spill over into telling others about the Lord? If not, it will certainly grow stale on us.

The helper

The third word, *diakonos*, means helper. Our word deacon is derived from it. In the New Testament it is widely used for practical help of all kinds. It describes our relationship both to those who are fellow Christians and to those who are not (2 Corinthians 4:5). Prison visiting and personal service (Philemon 13; Acts 19:22), handing out the soup and preaching, are all called by this word "service" (Acts 6:1, 4). Since the coming of Jesus into the world we can no longer insulate the sacred from the secular.

"This is how one should regard us, as servants of Christ" (RSV, 1 Corinthians 4:1). Ask yourself what difference becoming a Christian has made to you in the area of wholeheartedness, worship, and practical service. Ask the Lord what service he looks for from you.

Verse of Scripture to Learn

"THEREFORE, I URGE YOU,

BROTHERS AND SISTERS, IN VIEW

OF GOD'S MERCY, TO OFFER YOUR

BODIES AS A LIVING SACRIFICE,

HOLY AND PLEASING TO GOD –

THIS IS YOUR TRUE AND PROPER

WORSHIP."

(ROMANS 12:1)

Bible study: Servants of the Lord

The Bible study passage tonight is Acts 5:40 – 6:8.

1. What motivated these people to want to serve the Lord? How about you?

2. How many types of service are mentioned here?

3. Are the "spiritual" jobs more important than the practical ones?

4. What spiritual qualifications were required of those who wanted to serve lunches? Apply this to your group or church.

5. How was it that the disciples "multiplied" in Jerusalem?

6. What service are you now engaged in, or contemplating, which you would not have done before becoming a Christian?

7.	What new area of fellowship and service is each of you going to commit yourselves to now that this short course has ended? Be specific!

Prayer time

Members of the group should share with one another the areas in which they feel themselves called to serve Jesus, and pray for one another as they move from this group to new areas of fellowship and service.

> *"This is not the end. It is not even the beginning of the end. But it is the end of the beginning."*
>
> *Winston Churchill*

Session Notes

Session Notes

Tailpiece

There are three areas to remember as you leave the group.

1.Getting started

There are three sides to becoming a Christian. There's the personal side, as we repent and put our trust in Jesus. There's the divine side, as he welcomes us into the family and gives us the Holy Spirit to inhabit our personalities. And there is the public side, baptism.

We have not looked much at **baptism**, but it is very important. It is the mark of the Christian. If you quietly believe in Jesus in some Muslim countries nobody will bother you. But if you get baptized your life will be in danger. Baptism is the defining mark of belonging to Christ.

Nowhere does the Bible tell us the minimum age for baptism. It never tells us how much water is required. Sadly those two areas that the Bible does not even mention have caused an immense divide among believers. Everyone agrees that baptism is the mark both of God's welcome and of our response, but some denominations put the emphasis on the divine welcome and therefore baptize the children of believers, just as under the old covenant boys were circumcised as babies if born into a believing Jewish family. Other denominations put the stress on our response, and want to keep baptism for the public profession of faith in Christ by the believer. There is no doubt that a public baptism has a powerful effect, not only among those who witness it, but also on the candidates themselves.

Well, we are not going to be able to solve this centuries old division of opinion. But we can go some way towards it. If you have never been baptized and are now a committed Christian, then you need to complete your initiation by taking a public stand in baptism. And it will be a great blessing to you to nail your colours to the mast in this way.

If you were baptized as a baby you do not need to be baptized again. What was missing was your public acceptance of the grace of God held out to you in baptism. So you need to arrange with the minister in your church to have a public declaration of your commitment to Jesus. Some people find it helpful to go down into the baptismal waters again in memory of their baptism. But let's be clear on this. You can't be baptized twice any more than you can be born twice. Baptism means beginning. It is God's gracious seal on his acceptance of us and our acceptance of him. It is also a great encouragement when our faith runs dim. Even Martin Luther, that great champion of justification by faith, would recall when doubts assailed him, *baptizatus sum*, "I have been baptized!"

2. Keeping going

One of the saddest sights is to meet someone who began the Christian life well but has fallen by the wayside. We make a great enemy in the devil once we make a great friend of Jesus, and the devil is out to get us if he can. Sometimes it is by engaging in behaviour forbidden in Scripture. Sometimes it is through encouraging wrong habits we can't break. Sometimes it is through a relationship we ought never to have got involved in. One way and another, some fall by the wayside. Perhaps the most common reason is that we give up on spending time with the Lord. Our prayers gradually disappear. The Bible collects dust on the shelf. Communication has broken down. That is why it is so important to make time for a daily meeting with the Lord, so that he can reach us through the Bible and we can reach him through prayer. Here is a pattern you might care to adopt in conjunction with Bible-reading notes I mentioned earlier, which you can get either from the Scripture Union or the Bible Reading Fellowship. Christians often call it the quiet time.

The daily time

If we are to grow in our relationship with the Lord we need to be disciplined about a daily time with him. Regularity is more important than length!

Turn to God

Find a place to be alone, set aside everything else, and concentrate on God, who loves you and wants to deepen relations with you. Ask him to meet with you. The start of the day may be the best time, even if we are not "morning people"! It is useful to have a notebook with you as well as your Bible.

Turn to the Bible

Using your Bible-reading notes, open the Bible at today's passage. Read it twice – first to get the feel of it, then start looking more closely at it. Do not turn straight to the notes with other people's thoughts! Here are some useful questions:

- Is there anything here about God the Father, Jesus, or the Holy Spirit?

- What does it show me about human nature?

- Is there an example to follow or a mistake to avoid?

- Is there a command to obey or a warning to heed?

- Is there a promise to claim or a prayer I can use for myself?

- Is there a verse I want to learn, now or later?

- How can I apply this to my daily life?

- What one thought will I take away to reflect on at odd moments today?

Turn to your notebook

A notebook is useful. You can jot down some of the best thoughts you have had, and any specific prayers so that you can revisit them when they have been answered. Use your notebook to make a list of people or concerns you want to talk to God about occasionally or regularly. Write down the names of a few friends you long to become Christians.

Turn to your Bible-reading notes

See if they add anything to your own discoveries – but do your own discovering first!

Turn to prayer

Talk silently or aloud to Jesus, your friend. Talk about the things you have noticed in your Bible reading. Then turn to personal matters, family, friends, work, the needs of the church and the world. Don't forget to thank him for blessing you have received. And then commit the day to the Lord and get up and go on your way rejoicing.

The Sunday time

The other crucial way to keep going is to make the most of Christian fellowship. We are not meant to be lone rangers, but brothers and sisters in a family. So make sure of two things. One, that you find and go regularly to a lively church where the Bible is taught and where members really do love one another. There will probably be a variety of services for you to choose from, but second, make sure you include *the Holy Communion* or *Lord's Supper*. Like baptism the Communion is a physical mark of his love to us. But whereas baptism is once and for all, the Communion is God's loving feast along the way, often to be repeated. Paul, writing to new Christians at Corinth, helps us to make the most of it (1 Corinthians 10 and 11). He encourages us to:

- look back (11:23) to the cross where Jesus gave himself for you – in gratitude

- look in (11:28) and see what needs confessing – in repentance

- look up (10:16) and feed on him in your heart – by faith

- look round (10:17) to other worshippers – in fellowship

- look forward (11:26) to the messianic banquet in heaven – with joy.

3. Reaching out

If we don't give our faith away we are in danger of losing it. We can reach out in lots of ways – by our language, our behaviour, our generosity, the letters we write, and the invitations we offer. If we have found treasure we naturally will want to share it. Christians who keep their faith to themselves and never go public or go practical about it don't last the course.

In the Holy Land there are two large lakes. One is the Sea of Galilee and that is fresh, alive, full of fish. Why? Because the water flows into it, replenishing it, and also flows out of it, fertilizing the land below. The other great lake is the Dead Sea. It really is dead. Nothing lives in it, and it does not go anywhere. Why? Because water flows into it, but never flows out. If you want to make a success of your Christian life, resolve to be like the Sea of Galilee and not the Dead Sea.

Go with Jesus. Go well!

Photocopiable Material for Participants

The following pages can by photocopied and handed out to the participants in your group for use during the study.

Week One: Starting Out as a Christian

Real Christianity is not about churchgoing, creeds, conduct, or ceremonies – though it involves them all. Real Christianity is a relationship with Christ.

Jesus was not a mythical character like Santa, but a real historical person. He divides BC from AD. See Tacitus' *Annals* 15.44 or Josephus' *Antiquities* 18.3 for secular writers who attest his birth, teaching, execution by the Romans, the rumour of his resurrection, and the start of the church.

Hints as to his identity come in the two names given him at his birth: Emmanuel ("God is with us") and Jesus ("God to the rescue"). Truly human, yet his fulfilment of countless prophecies, the authority of his teaching, the character of his life, his claims (to forgive sins, accept worship, and be the world's final judge), coupled with his life of love and healing, his sacrificial death, and his wonderful resurrection combined to persuade many that God had indeed come among them.

He came to deal with our alienation from God. In his holiness God cannot accept our guilt and rebellion. In his love he took responsibility for it himself on the cross. Just before he died Jesus cried, "It is finished." The job of reconciling us to God was complete. His resurrection got the church started. He died to carry the guilt of human sin. He lives to break its power. More, his resurrection released him from the confines of a human body so that his Spirit could come into the lives of those who trust him.

How do I get in touch? It is as simple as ABCD.

A. There is something to *admit* – that we are estranged from God (Isaiah 59:1, 2; Ephesians 2:2) and are slaves to self-centredness (John 8:34). Even if we could live a perfect life from now on the past would still dog us (Romans 3:10). In order to get started we need to recognize this and be willing for change.

B. There is something to *believe*. Namely that Jesus has done all that is necessary to bring us back to God. His death dealt with our sins, and his risen life makes a new life for us possible (John 8:36).

C. There is something to *consider* – the cost of discipleship. Although the entrance fee for the Christian life is free (Jesus has paid it) the annual subscription is all we have got. We cannot serve God and the god of materialism (Matthew 6:24). We need to be willing to go public (Romans 10:9–10) and get into Christian fellowship. There will be opposition to face, as well.

D. There is something to *do* – to accept the gift that is Jesus. He says, "Here I am! I stand at the door and knock. If anyone hears my voice and opens the door, I will come in" (Revelation 3:20). He is excluded from our lives until we ask him in. But if we do, he promises he will come in. And he does not break his word. If you have genuinely asked him then he *has* come in and soon change will be evident.

Verse of Scripture to learn: "Here I am! I stand at the door and knock. If anyone hears my voice and opens the door, I will come in" (Revelation 3:20).

Bible study: Zacchaeus the Tax Collector: Luke 19:1–10.

Stimulating questions

1. Why do you think Zacchaeus felt the need to meet Jesus? Why do we?

2. Why did Jesus bother about the disreputable Zacchaeus?

3. Did Zacchaeus have to smarten up his life before Jesus would enter his home?

4. What does Jesus bring when he comes into someone's life?

5. What difference did Jesus' visit make to Zacchaeus?

Week Two: How Can I Be Sure I Am A Christian?

When we put our trust in Jesus we need to know where we stand. Can we be sure of him? Such doubts are common in the early stages of discipleship, and we need to deal with them. You cannot build a solid house on shifting foundations, or a Christian life if you are unsure whether you belong or not.

Scripture anticipates our doubts and answers them.

- Can I be sure I am accepted? Yes (John 6:37).
- Will God hold past failures against me? No (Romans 8:1).
- When I fail, do I lose my place in the family? No, but I need to repent (1 John 1:9).
- Can I keep it up? No, but Jesus can keep me up! (2 Corinthians 12:9)
- How can I overcome temptation? (1 Corinthians 10:13)

Our assurance is so important that the whole Trinity has got involved, and the first letter of John (1 John) tells us all about it. We can rely on:

The Word of God the Father

1 John 5:10–12 is powerful. If we believe human testimony, we can believe God's. It is ridiculous to accuse him of lying. His testimony is that he has given us eternal life, and that life is [all wrapped up] in his Son. If we have the Son, we have life. If not, we don't. That makes sense. How does a student know whether they are accepted at their chosen university? Because they have a letter from the competent authority assuring them they have a place. They may not feel they deserve it. But they are accepted on the word of the university. We need to hold on to the Word of God the competent authority.

The work of God the Son

The work of Christ, supremely on the cross, cancels our sins and makes access to God possible. "He is the atoning sacrifice for our sins, and not for ours only but for the sins of the whole world" (RSV, 2:2, and see 4:10). It is important to be clear on this, or discouragement can set in when new believers find their habitual failures have not yet disappeared. Our debts have been paid – once for all.

The witness of God the Holy Spirit

"This is how we know that he lives in us: We know it by the Spirit he gave us" (3:24). And the indwelling Holy Spirit shows himself gradually in many new ways. There will be a new desire to please God (2:5), a new assurance of pardon when we fail (1:9; 2:1–2), a new willingness to face opposition for our convictions (3:13), a new delight in the company of fellow Christians (3:14), a new generosity to people in need (3:17), a new experience of victory over temptation (4:4; 5:4), a new discovery of prayer getting answered (3:22; 5:14), and a new understanding and set of priorities (5:20–21).

God means us to *know* (not merely to hope or think) that once we have come to Christ we are permanently welcome in the Father's house. "I write these things to you who believe on the name of the Son of God that you may *know* that you have eternal life" (ESV, 5:13).

Verse of Scripture to learn: "He who has the Son has life; he who does not have the Son of God does not have life" (NKJV, 1 John 5:12).

Bible study: Saul's conversion: Acts 9:1–22.

Stimulating questions

1. Saul of Tarsus (later known as Paul) was intelligent, religious, virtuous, enthusiastic, and sincere. Surely such a man needs no conversion, then or now?

2. Later on in his life, Paul called his conversion "an example" (1 Timothy 1:16). In what ways is this true?

3. Was there any "Ananias" to help you in your discovery of Jesus?

4. What differences began to be seen in Saul's life that convinced him and others that the change was real?

Prayer time: God has no dumb children. He wants us to talk to him, naturally. So choose one thing you have learned this evening, or one verse that has struck you, and in a short sentence thank the Lord for it or ask for it to become real in your life. Praying out loud may seem strange to start with but it enables others to join with us and gets us used to putting our prayers into words.

Week Three: How Can I Grow My Relationship with Jesus?

Two great ways of developing a relationship with someone you cannot see are by letter (or email), and phone (or skype). It is like that with the Lord. The Bible is his letter to us; prayer is the phone.

The Bible

What is it? Not so much a book as a library with sixty-six books, forty authors in three languages written over 1,000 years. It contains many literary genres. But behind the human authors God was revealing himself and inspiring their message (2 Timothy 3:14–17; 2 Peter 1:21). Progressively it shows us what God is like and how we are called to live. The centrepiece is Jesus. The Old Testament points forward to him, the Letters look back.

Why read it? It is like a mirror to show us what we are like (James 1:22–25). It is milk for young Christians and meat for the mature (1 Peter 2:2; Hebrews 5:12–14). It can clean us up, guide us, and give us wisdom (Psalm 119:105, 165). It is a prime way of keeping in touch with Jesus (John 15:7).

How do we read it? Get a NIV version (or a Good News Bible) and a regular scheme for daily readings with some helpful notes, as provided by Scripture Union or Bible Reading Fellowship.

Wandering thoughts. How are we to handle them as we read? Turn the wandering thought into a short prayer and return to what you were reading previously.

Prayer

Prayer is crucial for developing the friendship. It has many aspects:
- Praise – appreciating God for who he is (Psalm 96:7–8).
- Confession – getting rid of the blockages (Psalm 32:3–5).
- Meditation – reflection on a Bible passage (Psalm 119:48).
- Thanks – for his gifts, his answers to prayer (Psalm 103:1–5).
- Requests – for others and ourselves (Matthew 7:7; 1 Thessalonians 5:25).
- Listening – does he want to tell us something? (Romans 8:26)
- Offering – ourselves for his service (Romans 12:1–2).

Learning to pray. We learn by doing it! Set a regular daily time (Daniel

6:10), pray alone (Mark 1:35), and with others (Matthew 18:20). Pray brief "arrow" prayers as need arises (Nehemiah 2:4–5 and Matthew 14.30). We learn from Jesus, starting with his pattern prayer (Luke 11:1–13) and then on to his meditation in John 17.

Unanswered prayer. When this happens we should ask ourselves some questions. Do we actually pray (James 4:2)? Did we really mean it (Matthew 7:7)? Are our goals selfish? (James 4:3). Is there unconfessed sin in the way (James 4:8)? Do we persevere in prayer (Luke 18:1–8)? Are we seeking our will rather than God's (Mark 14:36)? Answers do not always come in the form we expect. We may sometimes need to answer our own prayers (Matthew 14:15–16). The answer may be God's "no" or "wait".

Verse of Scripture to learn: "Your word is a lamp for my feet, a light on my path" (Psalm 119:105).

Bible study: Thanksgiving and prayer Colossians 1:3–24 or Acts 8:26–40.

Stimulating questions on Colossians 1:3–24

1. What are the main things for which Paul thanks God in the lives of these people he had never met?

2. Why is thanksgiving such an important part of prayer?

3. Paul is not slow to ask God for things in prayer. What sort of things? And how should we pray for our friends?

4. Paul prays that they may know God's power; what sort of things is that power to do?

5. What are the main marks of Christian discipleship in this passage?

Stimulating questions on Acts 8:26–40

1. What was the traveller doing as he rode along? Why did he need help?

2. How exactly did Philip help him? What might be the modern equivalent of the help Philip offered?

3. What effect should a fresh understanding of the Bible have on us as we expose ourselves to it?

4. Where does the Holy Spirit come into all this?

Prayer time: Take a verse from the passage and turn it into a prayer for yourself and then for a friend. Thank God for what has struck you tonight.

Week Four: How Can I Discover Christian Fellowship?

We start the Christian life on our own, but then discover we are in a new family – the church.

The nature of the church. The church has a bad image among some, but in reality is exciting. It is God's family (Galatians 4:4–7), Christ's bride (2 Corinthians 11:1–3), the Spirit's temple (Ephesians 2:19–22). It is a colony of heaven (Philippians 3:20), the body of Christ (Ephesians 4:15–16), and the army of God (Ephesians 6:12–20).

The job of the church is threefold: to worship God, to have fellowship with one another, and to offer service and witness to society (1 Peter 2:1–12 embraces all three).

The unity of the church. Jesus prayed for it (John 17:20–21), and they managed it, more or less, in the early days. But later human frailty and particular emphases led to denominations. God hates division in his people. Despite all appearances there is a God-given spiritual unity among all believers (Ephesians 4:4–6). We must seek to preserve and regain that unity.

The church – a classless society. The New Testament knows nothing about a clergy-laity division, nor about denominations. It is clear that nominal membership is not enough. It is a one-class society transcending all barriers (Galatians 3:28; Ephesians 2:14–18). It knows no different status among Christians, only different functions (Ephesians 4:11–12). Love is the bond to unite us.

The church's paradoxical character. It is both universal (Matthew 16:18) and local (Colossians 1:2). It is invisible but has visible expressions. Repentance and faith are the way into God's invisible church (1 Peter 2:4–5) and baptism is the mark of belonging to the visible church. But outward belonging does not always guarantee inner commitment. Many have the outward mark of baptism but no spiritual life.

The church's sacraments. Jesus left two physical marks for his new community. Baptism is the unrepeatable entry rite (Matthew 28:19) and the Holy Communion is the regular family meal for us to draw on his support together. It is a foretaste of heaven (1 Corinthians 11:23–26). We need both sacraments. If you are not baptized, go and talk to your minister!

Informal fellowship in homes, pubs, and sports. It is natural for birds of a feather to flock together!

Verse of scripture to learn: "Now you are the body of Christ, and each one of you is a part of it" (1 Corinthians 12:27).

Bible study: Sacrifice and service Romans 12:1–13.

Stimulating questions

1. What does true worship involve?

2. The church is Christ's body on earth. What implications flow from that? Do you see them in your local church?

3. If "each member belongs to all the others" (verse 5) what does this mean for our relationships?

4. According to Paul we all have different gifts and abilities. What main gifts does each of you think you have? What do others in the group think you have? How are your gifts being used for the common good in your church or college group?

5. See what this passage has to say about the practical fruits that flow from wholehearted surrender to Jesus. Is anything holding you back from presenting your body "as a living sacrifice?"

Prayer time: Get into pairs and pray over the use of each other's gifts. Then pray for one thing you would love to see happen in your church or Christian group.

Week Five: How Can I Experience the Holy Spirit?

The Holy Spirit is God: the eternal life of God active in our world. He was there at the start of everything (Genesis 1:2–3; 2:7) and in OT days was given to special leaders. But they looked for the coming of the Messiah when the Spirit would be widely available (Ezekiel 36:25–27; Jeremiah 31:31–34). Jesus was uniquely filled with the Spirit (John 1:32). He promised that after his death the Spirit, his "other self", would enter the lives of believers and empower them (John 14:15–18). That happened at Pentecost (Acts 2). Since then the Spirit is available for all believers.

The fruit of the Spirit. The Holy Spirit enters our lives at conversion (Galatians 4:6) and then begins to grow lovely fruit in our lives: love, joy, peace, and so on (Galatians 5:22–24). As we abide in Christ the vine (John 15:1–15), the Spirit rises like sap and produces the fruit we cannot personally create. So let's not grieve or quench the Spirit (Ephesians 4:30; 1 Thessalonians 5:10).

The gifts of the Spirit. The Spirit is a great giver. He equips God's people for life and service. Some examples of these gifts are in 1 Corinthians 12:4–13 and Romans 12:3–13. His supreme aim is to make us like Christ (2 Corinthians 3:18).

The power of the Spirit in temptation. Temptation comes to us all through "the world" (society which leaves God out – 1 John 2:15–16), "the flesh" (our own fallen nature – Romans 7:21–23) and "the devil" (the anti-God force of evil – 1 Thessalonians 3:5). Jesus clearly believed in the devil (Matthew 4:1–11) and experience points the same way (1 Peter 5:8–9). Jesus was tempted more than any of us, but never fell. He won the war, so he can help us with our smaller battles (Hebrews 2:18). He does so through the power of his Spirit in us (Romans 8:11–13, Galatians 5:16).

Victory secrets. There is always a way through temptation, if we will take it (1 Corinthians 10:13). Call at once on the Spirit's aid when temptation comes. Don't play with temptation. Don't flirt with "the world" – society, films, books, the web, and ambitions that dull your love for Christ. Don't spare "the flesh", that selfish "me" which needs daily crucifixion (Galatians 2:20; Romans 8:13). Don't compromise with "the devil". Resist him

(1 Peter 5:9) and avoid his favourite areas, like illicit sex, drunkenness, and the occult. A half-hearted Christian life is miserable and a poor example.

Verse of Scripture to learn: "I can do all things through him who strengthens me" (NRSV, Philippians 4:13).

Bible study: Spiritual gifts 1 Corinthians 12:1–13 or Genesis 3.

Stimulating questions on 1 Corinthians 12:1–13

1. How does verse 3 link Jesus with the Holy Spirit?

2. What do you learn from the variety of gifts and their unified source?

3. What do verses 8–10 teach about the kind of ministries we should be exercising in our churches?

4. What is meant by being "given the one Spirit to drink"? See John 7:37–39.

5. Does this passage give any support to the idea that there are two kinds of Christians – ordinary and "Spirit-filled"?

6. Will you ask the Spirit to fill you and equip you for service with whatever gifts he sees to be needed? "Ask and you will receive, and your joy will be complete."

Stimulating questions on Genesis 3

1. What was the prime cause of mankind's fall from grace?

2. What was the devil's supreme aim?

3. Why did he succeed?

4. What did the man and the woman hope to gain?

5. What were the consequences of yielding to temptation?

6. What hint is there of God's ultimate victory?

Prayer time: Write down two things you want the Spirit to do in you. Share them with the group, if you wish, and pray for one another

Week Six: How Can I Be Useful to God?

Two main ways: witness and service.

Witness

We do not join the army or police without putting on the uniform. It is the same in the Christian life. We are not to be ashamed of our allegiance. At Pentecost it was Peter who preached, but all of the disciples bore witness (Acts 2:32). Romans 10:9–10 stresses the need for unashamed witness. In many Muslim countries this could cost you your life. It is shameful that in the West we are so timid. In the NT "witness" always refers to witnessing to Jesus, not just talking about our own experience. How can people know we belong to Jesus unless we say so? So let's do that right now in this group where we know each other well – as a kind of "dummy run".

Service

The whole ministry of Jesus was one of service (Mark 10:45). That was his leadership pattern and he asked his followers to do the same (John 13:12–17). We are all ministers of Jesus Christ. The NT has three main words for "servant" or "minister". We are called to all three.

The slave, doulos (Greek). See 1 Peter 2:16: Revelation 1:1. It speaks of total ownership by Jesus. Ponder Romans 12:1–2 and 1 Corinthians 6:19–20. A slave in the ancient world had no money, no rights. Yet the NT deliberately and shockingly uses this word for Christians.

The worship leader, leitourgos. We get our word "liturgy" from it. It speaks of our worship (Acts 13:2). It is a big word and is used of our giving (2 Corinthians 9:12), our faith (Philippians 2:7), our job (Romans 13:6), our evangelism (Romans 15:16). Does our worship spill over into telling others about the Lord? If not it will grow stale.

The helper, diakonos – our *"deacon"*. Widely used in the NT of practical help of all kinds, including prison visiting and personal service (Philemon 13; Acts 19:22), the work of the chef and the preacher (both called "service" Acts 6:1, 4). Since the coming of Jesus into the world we can no longer separate sacred from secular. "This is how one should regard us, as servants of Christ" (RSV, 1 Corinthians 4:1). Go for it, and ask God what service he asks of you!

Verse of scripture to learn: "Therefore, I urge you, brothers and sisters, in view of God's mercy, to offer your bodies as a living sacrifice, holy and pleasing to God – this is your true and proper worship" (Romans 12:1).

Bible study: Servants of the Lord Acts 5:40 – 6:8.

Stimulating questions

1. What motivated these people to want to serve the Lord? How about you?

2. How many types of service are mentioned here?

3. Are the "spiritual" jobs more important than the practical ones?

4. What spiritual qualifications were required of those who wanted to serve lunches? Apply this to your group or church.

5. How was it that the disciples "multiplied" in Jerusalem?

6. What service are you now engaged in, or contemplating, which you would not have done before becoming a Christian?

7. What new area of fellowship and service is each of you going to commit yourselves to now that this short course has ended? Be specific!

Prayer time: Share with the group the area of service you feel called to and pray for one another as you leave this group for new areas of fellowship and service.

"This is not the end. It is not even the beginning of the end. But it is the end of the beginning."

WINSTON CHURCHILL